Conversa

Direct Answers To Any Difficult Social Question You've Ever Had

By

Chad Collins

Table of Contents

Introduction

Don't you wish that you had some sort of hack to improve your social skills more easily? If you are like most people, you struggle with social interactions. You may feel comfortable and even totally outgoing around close friends and family, but you are not that way in every situation. Your lack of social skills has made life more challenging and you feel like an awkward failure. If only there was some easy way to become more social and likable....

Oh, wait, there is! There are actually countless social hacks that can elevate your conversations from banal and boring to dynamic and enriching. You can make friends more easily, get business partners more readily, and feel more confident about yourself with these hacks. You can navigate tricky social situations that get the best of you and avoid the awkwardness that brings you down. This book has dozens of hacks that can make your social life soar.

Why should you trust me? Well, I have been in your shoes. I was awkward and geeky at one point. When I got into a business role, I realized that my lack of social skills was holding me back. So, I embarked on a mission to improve my social skills. Years of research and practice have led me to build my business from the ground up, make several lasting friends, and even get married. Now I want to share my secret recipe for social success with you.

As you can see from my story, social skills are the key to your success in life. You will not get far if you continue to be awkward and drive people away. Building good relationships starts with having excellent conversations and convincing people that you are a likable person. Anyone can have social skills. You just have to learn them and apply them. The results will astonish you.

I promise that by the end of this book, you will be ten times more social. You will have better conversations, and you will start to make better connections with people. You will even be a better persuader and influencer, getting your way.

Don't put off learning social skills any longer. Start reading now to improve your relationships and build new relationships. You will be amazed at how opportunities open up and your happiness swells.

Part 1: Specific And Practical Conversation Hacks

When it comes to making new friends, finding new business partners, recruiting clients or investors, and dating, conversation is what starts it all. With the exception of your family members, everyone you meet starts out a stranger. A conversation can change them into important people in your life. In fact, if you think about it, every relationship (except with your immediate family members) started with a conversation.

A conversation is far more than an exchange of words. It is an exchange of information and emotion that helps you get to know someone and show that person who you are. That sets up the framework necessary for a relationship to start. Early on in the relationship, a series of conversations enable both parties to determine if the relationship is worth pursuing and what nature it will take.

Obviously, conversations are absolutely critical to forming relationships with others. If you want to get to know anyone besides yourself, you need to have conversations. But simple conversations about the weather are not going to create much of a connection. A deeper connection is possible with some conversational hacks that enable you to actually get to know someone and convince him or her that you are worth getting to know.

What does science have to say about conversations? A Princeton study has concluded that conversations are not just verbal exchanges, but rather a sync-up between two minds [1]. Different parts of the brain, including those parts involved in processing the meaning of language, will activate. Two people who share similar communication partners and ideas will have brain activity sync up, essentially causing them to think the same way. This allows for a smooth flow of communication that does not cease into awkwardness. If you create that sync with someone, naturally a bond forms that can become a relationship of some kind.

What is even more interesting is that distinctive coupling was found between the brains of people telling life stories and people listening [1]. That means that when you tell or listen to a story, you start the process of this "mind meld." The result is that you feel infinitely closer to the other person. Stories are crucial elements of every culture in the world, and of every conversation. Being able to listen and tell stories are critical factors in making relationships with others.

Creating a mind meld is your ultimate goal of any conversation. These simple yet powerful hacks are easy ways to start the process. Take conversations to the next level and make them mean something.

Don't Be A Stranger

Do you know the number one mistake people make in conversation? They don't initiate conversation.

Basically, they don't even try. And you already know the commonsensical wisdom that you if you don't even try, you can't succeed.

Think of the people in your life. You may have some people that you talk to every day. You know them well and you know the ins and outs of their lives. Then you have acquaintances that you speak to occasionally out of politeness. You have the people you speak to when you have to, such as co-workers. Then there are the not-so-distant strangers, the barista who serves you your morning cup and the garbage man who collects your trash. They are in your everyday life but you don't know much about them because you don't speak to them beyond the necessary few words for your transaction. And finally, there are distant strangers, people whom you have never met and probably never will again, such as the guy next to you on the bus or the woman behind you in line at the grocery store. In fact, I am willing to bet that most of the people in your life are people you barely speak to.

But what about all of these people you don't talk to? From the co-workers you keep at arm's length to the distant strangers, these are people with stories, things to say, and connections that could further your goals in life. You have no idea if one of them might have the potential to be your next best friend or your new business associate. You will never know unless you try to talk to them.

So, don't be a stranger! Strike up a conversation with the person next to you on the place or the person in line. Find out what they are doing, who they are, and whatever else they want to tell you. You might be amazed at how these people can open up opportunities for you or tell you great stories that stay with you for years to come.

One time on a train ride, I was focused on my book, ignoring everyone else. The gentleman sitting next to me did not say a word to me the whole ride. I eventually glanced up from my book long enough to see that he was wearing a shirt from a small coffee place I go to often. I decided to set my book aside and strike up a conversation with him. Not only was he my neighbor, but he was also an employee at my favorite coffee joint. He gave me a free ride home from the train stop, saving me money on a cab, and he told me he would toss me a discount on coffee if I ever came in on his shift. Now we see each other now and then and we always have a little conversation. Just by talking to this man, I was able to save money on transportation and coffee and make a friendly acquaintance with one of my neighbors.

The people around you have a lot to offer. But they will not always initiate conversations. You cannot hang back and expect people to come to you because people are not programmed to talk to strangers. If you make the effort to start the conversations, though, almost everyone will respond. Then you may just find an amazing new person to add to your circle. Talking to new people is the only way to make them notice you and start new relationships that you may never have started otherwise. You might really benefit from these people, more than you ever expect. The person who was a stranger on the train one day might just become someone you can't live without a few months later.

In a study on how people initiate conversations on public transit, the researcher, Ole Putz, developed two theories for how people start conversations: The first is that they relax the rule against talking openly with strangers if there is a disruption in travel [2]. For instance, if the subway breaks down or bad weather creates a delay in a flight, fellow passengers are free to grumble to each other about the disruption. This can start a conversation. The second theory is that people notice things about each other that they have in common, such as another person wearing a concert T-shirt for their favorite band [2]. The latter theory proved to be the most common reason that two strangers found connections on public transit [2]. These two things can enable complete strangers to talk.

Therefore, use this data to your advantage. Use a disruption in travel or some circumstantial occurrence as an excuse to start a conversation, such as commenting on the music playing in an elevator or remarking how bad the weather is. That is an acceptable way to start a conversation with a complete stranger.

Otherwise, observe the stranger for clues about him or her. If you recognize the book he is reading, comment on it and talk about the book. If you like her outfit, say so. These comments can break the ice and allow for a conversation.

Finding things in common makes a mind meld even more likely and possible [3]. Similar neural responses to things are indicators of friendship because people like having things in common. If your neurons start excitedly firing over model trains, you are more likely to bond with someone who also gets excited over that as well. Finding similar interests, hobbies, or even relating to each other about places that you have both been to make for excellent conversation. For instance, if someone's luggage says "Paris," you can ask, "Have you been to Paris?" When the person says yes, you can talk about your experience in Paris or how you have always wanted to go there. Right there you have something in common to talk about.

Another great way to bond with someone is recognizing some cultural similarity. Say you recognize their accent as being from your home town, or you know the foreign language they are speaking in. You can pipe up about how you once lived there or you know the language or you studied that language in school. Apply whatever cultural or linguistic commonality you both share. Finding members of your own culture or background often feels like finding a friend in a sea of strangers. It instantly bonds you both.

It may also be time to finally talk to that barista or server you see every day, that guy who rides your elevator every morning, or that neighbor you always pass in the hall. If you have multiple interactions with someone, the natural barriers against speaking to strangers are eroded and a conversation will be more natural, less awkward. You may also have more of a bond already due to the mere exposure effect, a scientific phenomenon where someone becomes more attractive to you the more often you see him or her [4]. Finally, you have more of an ice breaker since you see each other often. It can be a lot easier to finally ask someone you see every day, "So I see you around a lot. What's your name?"

Most people are shy, or at least reticent to talk to strangers. They are just as afraid of rejection as you are. And if you think about it, the odds of being rejected or brushed off by a stranger are higher than someone you know. Most people won't take that risk because they don't know if it's OK to talk to a stranger or how to break the ice. You can set them at ease by breaking the ice yourself. Then you allow them to feel comfortable talking to you and they like you more.

If you are rejected by a stranger, don't take it personally. Some people just don't feel like talking because they are busy, rushed, shy, or having a bad day. Some people are just rude and unfriendly. For every person who rejects you, there are probably two who will welcome a conversation with you. You won't know unless you find out. You can minimize your chances of rejection by reading someone's social cues. These social cues are usually obvious. A person who has his arms crossed and headphones in probably doesn't feel like talking. A person who is looking around or who makes eye contact with you and smiles is more likely to want to talk.

Maybe the stranger is not giving any social cues. In this case, test the waters by making eye contact first and smiling. If the person responds in kind, you can break the ice. If the person dodges your look, turns away, glares at you, or puts headphones in or pulls out a book, you should probably just not bother.

Ask Away

Many conversations can start by simply asking for something. Persuasion also works this way. If you want something, ask. You (almost) never get what you don't ask for. So, ask! You either end up in the same position you were already in or you end up much better off.

How To Get What You Want

If you want to get to know someone, just ask. Then you find out if the person reciprocates the interest. Asking to talk or asking questions to get to know someone will break the ice.

If you want something from someone, such as a favor,

then ask. The worst they can say is no. Your boss is not going to give you any vacation time unless you ask. You often have to state a need before someone can accommodate it. Remember that no one is a mind reader. No one will just hand you what you want, assuming that you want it. You have to make the need known.

For the longest time, I was terrified to ask my boss for a raise. I was so sure that he would fire me on the spot. One day, though, I heard another co-worker got a raise. I asked him how he did it and he said, "I just showed the boss what I've been doing for the company and asked if I could get a reward for my efforts." I realized then that I had to ask, because my boss wasn't going to just come up to me and offer me more money. So, I prepared a presentation proving my value to the company and then I summoned the courage and asked him for some time. After my presentation, I asked for my raise. And guess what? He said yes. He never would have given me a raise otherwise. He didn't even realize that I wanted one because he is not a mind reader.

Asking is the first step. But it doesn't guarantee you what you want. You may have to push further and use some persuasion. Persuasion is a huge subject beyond the scope of this book, but there are a few basics that you should always use.

The first is proving how getting what you want benefits someone. If you're asking a girl out, for instance, show her how she will enjoy time with you and what you can do for her on the date. Or if you are asking for raise, show how you deserve it and how a raise will keep you invested in your work. Focus on the other person's benefit, not your own. No one cares about how you will benefit. They only care about what they get from it. Prove that someone will get something from doing what you want and you will probably get approval.

You must always make someone feel motivated to

want to help you. No one is going to do something for you unless they have a valid buy-in. You can do this one of two ways: get someone to like you or use Maslow's Hierarchy of Needs for motivation.

The principle of getting someone to like you was first proposed by Dr. Robert Cialdini in his famous six principles of influence. If you make someone feel that they like you, then they want to do favors for you [5]. Another Cialdini principle is called reciprocity, wherein you do someone a favor to get one in return [5]. Create a you-scratch-my-back-I-scratch-yours situation. The person likes you for doing him favors and benefiting him so he is inclined to do the same for you.

Maslow's Hierarchy of Needs involves appealing to someone's needs on a scale [6]. People are motivated by how they perceive their needs will be met by you. If someone sees a way to benefit from helping you with minimal cost to him- or herself, then he or she will gladly do it. The hierarchy starts with basic needs for survival – food, water, shelter. Most people in Western countries have these needs met, but you may find that offering to buy someone food or giving someone a place to stay can motivate them to help you out somehow.

The second level involves the need to feel safe [6]. Improving someone's sense of safety may be as simple as defending them from bullying or promising to keep a secret safe. You can offer someone emotional security by reassuring them about how well they are doing or praising them.

The next level is the need to feel as if they belong and are loved [6]. Offering someone friendship is a good way to get them to want to help you because you are satisfying this need. People want to be liked. If you make someone feel that you will like them more in exchange for a favor, then you may just have your in. However, this usually doesn't work on secure people who already have high self-esteem because such people do not require your approval to feel good about themselves. It only works on insecure people who make it clear that they are desperate for friends or people who admire you and seek your friendship.

Esteem is the third need. This is where someone needs to feel valued and good about themselves. Flattery and praise play in here. Telling someone that he is doing a great job can motivate him to want to do an even better job by helping you. In fact, it has been found that when you praise someone, they are more likely to try to please you to get more praise [7]. In a study, students complimented women who wore blue to class, and noticed that the number of women wearing blue went from 25% to 38% [7]. Then they started complimenting those wearing red and the number of women wearing red skyrocketed 11% to 22% [7]. If you praise someone, they will repeat the behavior and try to keep getting praise. You can incur their compliance simply by complimenting them.

Plus, it has been found that people really can't tell between sincere and insincere flattery [8]. A study of people who used flattery in the workplace showed that they were rated as more competent and better at their jobs than those who did not use flattery, regardless of how sincere the flattery was [8]. Any form of praise works. You can mean it or not mean it, but act like you mean it. For instance, if you want to flatter your least favorite co-worker, you may struggle to find things that you sincerely appreciate about her, so point out something that she values highly. You might praise her organization abilities if she is a neat freak, for instance, since her habits indicate she cares highly about being tidy.

The final level is the need to be self-actualized or feeling like one is fulfilling his or her full potential in life [6]. People usually only focus on this need when they have satisfied their other needs. You can satisfy this need by telling someone how their efforts will further their career, help them help the community, or open new opportunities. You can also tell someone how he is in a great position to help you and he can really improve your life, playing to his power and how far he has gotten in life by his own work.

The second part of influence is showing someone that they will suffer little cost from helping you, or that the cost is worth the benefit. Asking something from anyone poses a problem, in that they must expend some sort of effort or resource on you. Make this cost seem worthwhile. Usually, offering a person a large enough benefit is sufficient to cover the cost. But this is not always the case. As long as you make something seem easy and convenient, you can convince someone to do it.

The final part involves learning what you can about a person. Then you can appeal to something unique about him. For instance, if you have kids and your boss has kids, you might use the reason that you want more time to spend with your children to convince him to let you go home earlier. You might find out that someone hates being left out so you invite him to a party in exchange for a favor. The more you know about someone, the more bargaining power you have.

It is beneficial to find out what someone loves and what someone hates. You can use both in your bargaining. Show him how he can avoid what he hates or gets what he loves by helping you.

Drive Conversations Forward With Questions

Questions drive conversations forward. But while most books on this subject encourage you to ask lots of questions, you may find a repetitive list of questions in real life can feel more like an interrogation. Asking questions the right way is how you can get a conversation to move forward and gain interest from both parties.

First, set some clear guidelines for what makes a

question too personal. Really personal questions make people uncomfortable. You don't want to ask about someone's specific health concerns, for instance, or why someone got a divorce. People will share such information if they want. People have individual limitations on what they are comfortable discussing and what topics are taboo. You just have to get to know someone to find out what topics and questions are acceptable. Let the person guide you by listening to the details that he or she provides. Stop asking about something if the person seems to start fidgeting, looking away, or evading questions.

Second, avoid asking questions in rapid-fire succession. You want to take a more natural, calm approach. Ask a question, listen to the answer, and then think of your reply. Share something about yourself to find a common point of interest. For instance, ask someone if she has pets. When she says she has a cat, say that you love cats and then talk about your own cat. Be sure to share as much as you ask. Let the other person get to know you, too.

A great way to keep a conversation going is to ask someone for an explanation. If they say something that you don't understand, ask about it. If your new conversation partner mentions a band you have never heard of, ask what kind of music they play or even ask to hear a song. Find relevant questions to ask about what someone says. When you do this, you make a person feel as if you really care because you are listening and trying to learn more.

Say someone is an expert on something. There is no better way to start a relationship than to ask him or her about a subject within his or her expertise. For instance, at an art gallery opening, ask the art connoisseur about the art presented. You will not seem like a fool if you profess that you don't know something. Your eagerness to learn will make others want to teach you.

You can even ask people for advice to start a

conversation. But be sure to only ask if you intend on following the advice. No one likes to give advice only to have you argue with them. Ask someone for some input on a situation and then make them feel good by saying, "Thanks! That's great advice. You really helped me."

People all have opinions and they love sharing them. Asking someone's opinion will definitely break the ice. "What do you think of that performance?" is something you can ask someone you were sitting next to at a concert. "What did you think about that play?" can be a good ice-breaker at a game. "What do you think about this place?" is another example. Ask someone what they think and you will hear a reply.

If you can't ask an opinion relevant to a situation you are both in, then ask someone their opinion on current events. People love discussing current events. Since we are all in this life together, experiencing the same things differently, asking people about current events can offer you a wealth of perspectives. It can also shed light on someone's character and help you decide if you want to pursue a friendship or partnership with someone. For example, if you are opposed to a political candidate and someone else loves him, you might not want to push the relationship further because you have fundamental differences in how you feel about life.

One thing people love to do is to talk about their cultures. They appreciate others showing interest and trying to become educated. Don't assume you know everything about a culture just because you have been exposed to it on TV. If you meet someone of a cultural background different from your own, try to ask questions about their customs and beliefs. Ask, "What was it like growing up in that culture?" Never assume someone is foreign. Let the person tell you if he or she is from a different country and then ask about that country and what it is like living there. Don't state stereotypes or make jokes. Just try to learn what you can about said culture.

When you ask questions, try to find out what you share with someone. You want to drive the questions toward getting to know a person and what he or she may share with you. As you already know, commonalities bond people, so your ultimate aim is to find as many as you can. You want to ask about their hobbies, culture, and the like. You can also comment on things you notice about them, such as the book someone is reading on the train. Try to find out if you like the same pop culture icons or follow the same TV series.

Often, just by observing someone, you can come up with some questions to ask. "I see you have a lot of purple in your outfit. Is that your favorite color?" "I see that picture of a cat on your desk. Is that your kitty?" "I noticed that you only eat salads at lunch. Are you a vegetarian?" It is very flattering when you notice details about someone, and it shows you care if you ask questions relating to those details.

Paying attention to details helps you find things in common, too. "I love that team, too!" is an example of how you can break the ice if you see someone wearing a hat representing a specific team. "Who is your favorite player?" is a question you can ask to keep the conversation going.

Form Bonds Over Similar Situations

When you are in a situation with someone, you have a rich opportunity to bond over it. Two people trapped in a stuck elevator can become fast friends because they are sharing an experience that puts them in close proximity and exposes them to the same problems.

When you find yourself in a situation with someone else, use that situation to create conversation. You have a convenient ice breaker: a comment about the mutual situation. The other person is more likely to respond because he is sharing something with you and it would be awkward to not respond if you two are stuck together in the same place. Remember that Putz study about how strangers on a train tend to initiate conversations [2]? That's a prime look at how similar situations can form a bonding point.

Don't Be Selfish

We have all spoken to that selfish blowhard who goes on and on and on about himself or herself. You know how annoying it is. Yet you may do this yourself, simply because it is human nature to talk about yourself. You enjoy the sound of your own name the most, you enjoy talking about things you care about, and you enjoy stating your opinions. In your little world, you are the most important thing that exists; to others, maybe you're not so important, because they are preoccupied with themselves.

Most books on social skills suggest focusing on what other people want to talk about. This is great advice, in that other people will enjoy talking to you if they can talk about themselves, given the point above. Yet it makes for some dull conversations when you just don't care about what they have to say. And what about you? Don't you have the right to talk about yourself a bit and enjoy the conversation?

Well, yes, you will actually have better conversations if you talk about yourself a bit. The key here is finding a nice balance. You want to give and take. There are two kinds of communicators: those who share and those who ask questions [9]. Well, actually, there is a third type: the person who shares and ask questions. When rated on effectiveness, the third type tended to get the best scores [9].

The open sharer will think, "I feel like I'm being interrogated! Will this person ever tell me anything about himself?" when speaking to a question asker. The question asker thinks, "Wow, will this person ever ask me anything?" The two styles don't mix.

Therefore, blending them tends to remove that problem. You are not interrogating anyone and you are sharing things without seeming selfish.

So, basically, you want to ask questions to get the other person to share things about himself. You want to show an active and genuine interest, which looks like praise to the other person. And you want to listen well. But then you want to give some details about yourself too. Try to fit them in where they are relevant, such as agreeing with someone or sharing a story similar to the one someone else shared. You want to say, "I went through that too" or "I have a dog too."

Don't be selfish when it comes to conversation. Don't hog the spotlight for too long. A few minutes is the maximum amount of time you should hold the spotlight before giving it back to the other person. That way, you are sharing and letting the person get to know you, but you are not boring the person to death.

You also want to spread the love, so to speak. You want to promote and recognize others as much or even more than yourself. You come across as conceited and obnoxious when you are constantly self-promoting. If you spread the love a bit, you make others feel esteemed, which is one of Maslow's hierarchical motivators [6].

People love praise, plain and simple. In fact, so much so, that a study about the neural responses teenage girls have to maternal praise and criticism was astonishing: girls who hear criticism develop brain activity similar to depression and often go on to develop depression and anxiety issues as adults if they hear constant criticism [10]. People are hardwired to hate criticism and to love praise, so you want to dole out the praise.

How do you do this? It can be as simple as offering someone a compliment on her outfit. Or it can be more significant, such as praising someone's heroic efforts spearheading a donation campaign or someone's amazing contributions to the company. Tell someone how great or strong they are and give some real evidence as to why you think so. Tell the person, "We couldn't be here without you. Your work is so important." The flood of oxytocin and dopamine that someone gets from hearing such words will make them love you so much more.

The thing about doing this is that others will love the attention. Then they are likely to return the favor by the rule of reciprocity [5]. So, while you do something selfless by directing praise and attention toward the other person, you will likely benefit. Plus, you make the person feel good so that he or she will like you more. Then you can reap even more benefits from the relationship.

As long as your praise does not sound insincere, people will appreciate it. Realize that compliments less meaning with use, so repeating the same compliment or telling different people the same compliment makes its power wear out [8]. You want to give out unique compliments and at least try to make them sound genuine.

Flavor Your Conversation With Enthusiasm

When someone asks you how you're doing, answer with "Fantastic!" or "Super!" or "Wonderful!" instead of the usual "fine" or "good." These adjectives just sound better and will really engage the person you're talking to and others around you. Try it out and notice how people always have something to say if you say more than "Good."

I love to tell people that I'm doing fantastic. They perk up when they hear this. They say things like, "Why are you doing fantastic?" I just said something unusual that is also positive. It captures others' attention.

There are other ways to be enthusiastic, too. Say someone invites you out for drinks after work. "OK" with a glum face is not very comforting to the other person; it makes him think that you don't really want to meet up for drinks. But if you grin and say, "You bet!" then you seem more interested and that comforts the other person that you really want to spend time with him.

You want to always respond to others with enthusiasm. Respond to their questions and stories with keen interest. Say yes emphatically. Talk animatedly. Use more interesting words than the dreary ones like "OK" and "I guess" and "good."

Be Inspirational

One conversational hack is to inspire others. When you do this, you make others feel amazing, like the world is theirs for the taking. You goad people to act and feel confident. The result is that you make people like you because you give them that inspirational push to be better in life.

Being inspirational also helps you become a better public speaker. A bored audience is not going to feel the urge to act. A worked-up audience will. You want to inspire people when you talk as practice for when you might need to inspire an audience, give someone a pep talk, or even sell a product to a reluctant customer.

Inspiring an audience or a person is about helping them see *their* vision. Not yours. Your vision has little import for others, but if you speak to their visions, you are speaking in terms they can understand. Imagine if you are trying to inspire a group of people to sign a petition. Talking about how you believe in this cause and you want to see change won't mean much to others. But if you talk about how it will impact their lives and help them move forward, you make it clear why they should care. You can get them inspired to sign the petition if they see how they will benefit or how they will be responsible for bringing about the change they want to see in the world.

Dale Carnegie said it best: Dramatize your ideas [11]. Some showmanship is in order when you are inspiring others. Compare the difference between a dreary PowerPoint and a dynamic one. If you want people to care about what you have to say, then you want to make them *feel* something. Offer them an experience or show them shocking images or speak about the suffering of mankind. Carnegie uses the example of a rat poison company using a display with live rats to successfully boost their sales [11]. This is an example of how you do something to shock people and make an idea real to them so that they feel inspired.

The best way to inspire others is to find out their personal values. Most people tend to commit to something and then stick with it [5]. This principle is one of Cialdini's principles, called commitment and consistency. If you find out how your idea ties in with someone's personal values or causes, then you have an easier in.

It is also easy to inspire people in conversation by finding out their values. A friend who is down in the dumps about his girlfriend leaving may value long-term relationships, so you can inspire him to feel better by pointing out how the relationship benefited him and offered a learning experience to make him better in future relationships. Find out what someone cares about, then target that.

You will find this especially useful in business. If you are approaching an investor, you know that he cares about money above all. So, you want to inspire him to feel that his money is wisely spent on your venture.

When it comes to getting people to do what you want, refer back to some of the influence principles covered before, but also focus on praising these people and making them like you. Doing these things will inspire people to want to please you.

Flattery Will Get You Far

Praise will always motivate people more than criticism. Praise people for doing well and praise those who aren't likely to change. You may just see change in everyone if you offer praise.

Negative comments tend to stick more than positive ones [12]. If you tell someone that he can't succeed, that will stay with him forever. He will forever have a bad taste in his mouth about you because you discouraged him. If you tell someone that she is fat, she will never forget that and will always resent you at some level, no matter how forgiving of a person she tries to be. You make people feel with your words and they tend to remember those feelings for life. Using this knowledge, tread carefully when you speak to people and try to make them feel right.

The best way to make people like you and want to talk to you is to make them feel good with praise. Praise is a huge motivator that encourages people to stick with whatever it is they are doing. It may motivate them to try even harder, too. By praising people, you motivate them to hang out with you.

Use compliments selectively, though. You don't want to just say something like, "You lost a lot of weight!" The recipient may perceive that as an insult instead of a compliment. You don't want to use barbed compliments, which combine an insult with a compliment. Don't point out anything negative or how someone has done better than before. You just want to point out the positives now. Back to the "You've lost weight" compliment, try something more like, "You look great!"

The same old dreary words that everyone says don't have much of an impact. Telling a pretty woman that she looks good won't have as much weight as, "You look absolutely stunning tonight!" Pick words that are more dynamic and unique.

Try to be more specific. "You did great today" is vague. Instead, you want to point out just what you admire about the person's performance today. "I really admire how you reached your sales goal!" or "You really ran well" are examples of specific compliments. They have more meaning because they show a person just what you are complimenting.

Never second-guess what you said or keep adding words to it. Keep the compliment short and sweet. Then it seems more sincere. Going back on what you said, making a big flashy statement, or saying something like, "I think" or "I guess" will make your compliment seem insincere.

Giving the same compliment again and again won't do you any favors, either. Compliments lose steam with time. Instead, find ways to reword the same compliment if you must give it more than once. Otherwise, just give a compliment once and find a different compliment later on.

As a leader, your job is to motivate your followers. People will respond well to praise, no matter how insincere [8]. They are likely to make improvements in their performance in order to earn more praise. You can really motivate workers or team members by telling them that they are doing well, even if they are not. If you don't see the change you want, then you want to let these people go. They are just dragging the organization down and there is no way to motivate them if they don't care about being praised.

You should also praise people after a hard day. Maybe no one reached the goal, but they tried. Acknowledging that everyone tried can be a huge motivator that makes your team members or employees feel validated and more encouraged.

Acknowledge that something was hard and that everyone did their best.

When you have to criticize someone, start with praise to soften the blow. Use more vague terms and suggest ways that the person can improve. Don't just be rude or level accusations at someone. Generally, you don't ever need to criticize someone. Keep negative comments to yourself.

Gratitude Is The Best Form Of Flattery

You already know that flattery is effective at getting people to like you or try to please you, but flattery is not always about compliments. Sometimes showing gratitude for what someone has done is sufficient flattery [13]. Acknowledging what someone has done and showing appreciation is a form of praise that validates a person's efforts and makes them want to do more for you. A simple thank you is often all it takes.

Another trick is to send handwritten thank you notes to anyone who helps you, interviews you, or goes into business with you. It will make you stand out significantly and make the recipient feel much more valued. Something about the written word tends to make a greater impression on the human brain [14].

Always Do Follow-Ups

Marge tells you she has a doctor's appointment. The next time you see her, you ask how the appointment went. Marge is flattered that you remembered and cared enough to ask.

Always follow up on what people tell you. Attempt to remember fine details and bring them up later. People find this highly flattering. Your thoughtfulness shows you care, which makes people want to know you better.

A follow-up can be as simple as remembering that

someone is vegan and keeping that in mind when you suggest places to eat. It can involve remembering that someone has kids or when his birthday is. Always try to remember what you can.

Also, a follow-up can include touching base after you speak to someone. You exchange contact information and later on you ask them how they are doing or ask about something they mentioned in the conversation. Even just a, "It was nice meeting you!" is a thoughtful touch.

A conversation is the opening of a relationship. But the relationship won't happen if the interaction ends with the one conversation. You must push for a relationship by finding a way to stay in contact and then following up. Out of sight, out of mind is definitely real. You have to stay on someone's mind and make them continue to notice you to become part of that person's life.

Furthermore, repeated exposures and follow-ups make you more attractive to someone. The mere exposure effect refers to how someone finds you more attractive the more often he or she sees you. It is estimated that at least five exposures are required to make someone notice you and fifteen to make them find you the most attractive [4]. In one study, five random women who resembled each other attended a lecture at a university. One woman didn't go at all, one went once, one went five times, one went ten times, and so on. At the end of the lecture, students were asked to rate pictures of the women from least attractive to most attractive. The woman who had attended the most got the highest rating. To make someone like you, you must let them see you at least fifteen times.

Open-Ended Questions

Some questions are close-ended, meaning that they lead to only a yes or no answer. They don't invite discussion or detail. The conversation ends with that question, unless you want to ask another. Open-ended questions invite more discussion and keep the conversation going.

Consider the difference between these two questions:

"How was your day yesterday?"

"Good."

"What did you do yesterday?"

"We played volleyball and went to a barbecue place for dinner. We had the best ribs ever."

The first question is easy to dismiss with a monosyllable. But the second invites the person to share details that you can respond to. Always stick to questions that are open-ended because they keep the conversation going. Close-ended ones cause the conversation to die.

"Tell Me More"

This single phrase is one of the greatest conversation hacks in existence. Use it and use it often. When someone tells you something, smile and say, "Tell me more." Or some variation of that phrase. This invites the person to keep talking. It is also flattering, because it proves that you care and you are paying attention. Inviting a person to keep talking about something he or she is interested in causes the person to enjoy the conversation more.

The Emotional Contagion Of Conversation

Emotions are unbelievably contagious, even worse than the common cold [14]. The result of a Princeton study has concluded that the emotion you put out in conversation will affect others. Therefore, you can set the mood for a conversation. If you want people to feel good talking to you and to come back for more, well, you may just want to exude a cheerful and positive mood to make others happy. A gloomy mood will just bring everyone down.

The way you speak indicates your mood. If you are complaining, for instance, you project a gloomy or negative mood. The subjects you choose also affect the mood. Everyone around you will reflect that mood. Most people are not interested in standing there listening to someone complain, nor do they want to feel blue from a conversation about your dog dying.

If you want people to like you, you want to make them feel happy. This calls for more positive, happy talk. Talk about light subjects, share jokes and funny stories, and point out the positives in things. Being a positive person means that you are more pleasant to be around.

A lot of people with poor social skills will complain as a way to bond with others. If you complain, others may agree and commiserate with you. The issue here is that people with good social skills don't want to do that. They are in a more positive state of mind. Also, if you build a relationship entirely on commiseration, then you have created a negative and even toxic relationship that does not include much joy.

The secret is to at least pretend to be happy. That will come across in your language and body language. Then others will feel happy. Since people like feeling happy, it only makes sense that causing others joy will make them like you more.

Repeat What You Hear

Reflective listening is a conversation hack that therapists have mastered. It is a method by which you listen to someone and repeat back what they say. Of course, you want to paraphrase their point into one simple sentence. There are several benefits to this.

The first benefit is that you prove that you are

listening. You have absorbed everything the person said without losing the gist of the conversation. This makes the other person feel validated.

The second is that you can clear up misunderstandings this way. You repeat back what you gathered from the person and if you got it wrong, you just showed the person what you didn't get right. The other person now has a chance to correct you. Misunderstandings can be avoided this way and you can avoid working on assumptions. For instance, if someone seems mad and tells you that he is mad at you because of something you did, you can paraphrase it. Show him that you know why you made him mad so that you can avoid angering him in the future. If you missed the point, he will be able to correct you. Then you are able to avoid causing anger in the future.

The third benefit is that you can gather what someone is really feeling to form an emotional connection. You go beyond the words by paraphrasing what the person said and then saying, "You must feel [insert emotion]." The person can then correct you if you are wrong. You gain a better understanding of what the person feels and how the person reacts to certain life events. For instance, if someone is telling you how he was cheated on, you can say, "I am sure you feel very hurt." He can then say, "No, I just feel angry." You now know his true emotional state and he feels better because you understand him.

Always validate what someone says, too. "I would feel that way too" is a good way to validate someone. This is a tip especially useful when someone is venting to you or you are talking to a victim of a crime. It is a delicate way to handle victims because they already feel bad and you are letting them know that they are not overreacting.

Listen With Your Eyes

Half of a conversation is talking and the other half is

listening. In fact, it can be argued that listening is more important than talking. But listening is not just as simple as hearing what someone says and coming up with relevant responses. You need to pay attention to a variety of factors in the conversation.

Watch someone's body language. Does it match their words? A person who says she is fine while crying is obviously not fine, for example. You can notice discrepancies between words and body language and understand more about what the person is actually feeling.

You can also catch subtle social cues that people give. Few people want to be rude, so they might not say, "I don't want to talk about this." But you can tell they want to leave the topic or the conversation by the way they inch toward an exit, glance at the clock, or yawn. Then you can change the subject or politely excuse yourself so that the person doesn't hate you for trapping him or her in a boring conversation for hours.

You can also tell when someone is passionate about something or likes something. Their pupils will get bigger and their gestures grander. They will raise their voices. They will be more animated and excited, with faster breathing. You can tell they care about this topic so you can keep that in mind for the future.

Put Your Body Into It

Seeing how language is so much more than mere words, it makes sense that you need to put your body into your conversation. What you say with your facial expressions, body language, and tone is important.

People are listening with their eyes, too. Your body language is crucial in keeping the conversation going on a pleasant note. You can betray your real thoughts and emotions in body language, which can deter people from talking to you. You may also be giving mixed messages without intending to, which can kill a conversation rapidly too.

Often, people misinterpret your body language. You might be antsy because you are nervous, but someone else could think that you are not interested in the conversation. Be mindful of your body language and try to appear cool, calm, and confident.

The best body language hacks involve leaning toward someone as they speak. Touch them now and then, such as a light touch on the arm as you make a point or laugh together. Make eye contact but look away every twenty seconds to make it seem natural. Keep your body facing someone and keep your arms and legs uncrossed and open. Hold your head up high to show attention and interest. Smile a lot. Nod to validate what someone is saying.

One little trick to help you relax and have more confident body language is to chew gum. No one will think twice about why you are chewing gum but it will calm your nerves.

Talk To Someone Like He Is Already Your Friend

The difference between a conversation that remains cold and formal and one that turns into friendship is the warmth you exude. You can make people like you and feel closer to you if you always speak to them as if they are already your friends. Do this even with strangers to break down the barriers people set up between themselves.

How do you do this? The main key is to just be warm. Offer lots of compliments. Pat the person on the back or touch his arm. Laugh a lot and tell jokes. Share a bit about yourself. Talk easily and fluidly, and keep a relaxed, confident posture.

A study found that certain questions tend to bond people more quickly [16]. These questions are personal without being nosy or rude. There are fifty such questions, some of them being:

What did you want to be when you grew up?

What is your best memory?

What would you do if you found out you had a month left to live?

If you could live anywhere in the world, where would it be?

If you could have anyone in the world, living or dead, as a dinner guest, who would you choose?

What would be a perfect day for you?

Do you ever rehearse what you are going to say before

making a phone call? Is there a reason why you do this if you do?

What are you most grateful for in your life?

How would you choose to die, if you could choose?

What made you fall in love with your partner/spouse?

If you had the chance to learn your future, would you do it?

These questions are interesting and let you get to know someone. But they also erase the boundaries people have. In this study, conversation partners were asked to rate how close they felt to the other person [16]. The group that asked these questions rated a high level of closeness, while the group that made small talk rated a low level of closeness [16].

You can try this activity with someone. But you can also simply talk to them as if you know them. Don't say things like, "I don't know you but..." Say something more like, "You seem like the kind of person who would do this. Am I right?"

Speak about how you admire the person or how you feel grateful for something they have done. Express both praise and gratitude in one breath. This is what good friends do and you can do it with a stranger, too.

Be sure to talk as if you will see each other again. Say "I will see you later" instead of good-bye. Mention that you want to follow them on social media or get their number. Doing this allows you to follow up and give the impression that you want a real friendship to bud from this interaction.

Part 2: Conversational Situations

Have you ever had a conversation that took an unexpected turn or seemed resistant to the usual advice that social skills books give? You probably felt off-kilter and failed to respond correctly. As a result, the conversation ended on an awkward or even sour note and no relationship was born of it. Conversations are all unique and no two will go the same. Learning how to handle different situations is imperative to having good social skills.

This is the exciting part: real-life examples and applications for the hacks you learned in Part 1. A lot of books like this just throw theoretical ideas at you and expect you to figure out how to apply them in real life. This book is a little bit different in that you will see some real-life uses and situations that you are likely to encounter. These situations can throw you off, but after reading this part, you will know how to skillfully navigate them with a minimum of awkwardness and embarrassment.

How To Answer Questions With Information That Doesn't Lead To A Dead End

I'm sure you have encountered this scenario: Someone asks you a question, you answer, and that is that. What you have inadvertently done is create a dead end which halted further communication. Phrasing your answers the right way can prevent that from happening.

When someone asks you a question, avoid giving a yes or no answer. Yes or no does not give the other person much to respond to. They have to make the effort to think of something else to say, and many people won't make that effort. You also make people wonder if you even want to be talking. Monosyllables are characteristic of those who want to stop talking. Providing some details or a story in response to their question is better than offering a monosyllabic answer.

Also, be sure to follow their questions with a question

of your own. For instance, if someone asks, "How are you?" don't just say, "Fine!" Ask them how they are doing. Or if someone asks what team you like, don't just answer with your team, but also ask them what their team is.

You want to give detail, without rambling. Rambling is a symptom of pure nerves. It is common in people who don't know what to say. To avoid it, stick to the topic of the question. Use it as a springboard for relevant topics.

Center your answers around finding something in common with the other person. As he asks questions, he is trying to find out who you are. Show him and then find out who he is. Find things you can relate on. The topics he brings up and the questions he asks are likely related to the things he likes, so you have a solid clue about how to talk to him now.

Some people ask leading questions, which fish for the

right answer. This might be, "What do you think of this weather?" You know that you are supposed to reply, "Oh, it's nice, isn't it?" It may be useful to follow the lead to please the person. But the answer to a leading question can also lead to a dead end, since you don't know what else to say. So, you may switch things up by replying to the leading question with an unexpected answer. This will throw the other person off and make him ask you for more information about why you said what you did. "It's nice, but I like the rain better," could be an example of this.

Learn when to cut in and end rambling, too. When the person takes a breath, you can cut in with something relevant or a question of your own. That way, you are locked in a mono-conversation, where one person does all the talking, often out of nerves.

Dealing With Awkward Silences In Conversations

Don't you hate it when you are talking to someone and then one of you says something that leads to a dead end? Now you're both stuck on this jammed elevator in awkward silence, or you're both on a date feeling really awkward. The thing is, silence creates a major sense of exclusion and pressure to speak [17]. But often both people feel scared to even speak and say something to make things more awkward. This spirals into saying nothing at all and the conversation is over.

First, relax and give it time. Conversations lull and lag naturally, and it's not always because you said something wrong. The other person needs time to think of a new tangent and to process what you have said. Give your partner a few seconds to a few minutes to collect his thoughts. If he really looks like he is not going to say anything, you can then cut in with a new tangent.

Sometimes, it is best to gracefully accept that the conversation is over. The person is done talking; you have exhausted your reserve of things to say to each other. Again, this may not be something personal. It is most common when talking to polite acquaintances or strangers. What needed to be said has been said. You will only make things more awkward by continuing to speak. Give it a few moments and then try to say something. If the awkwardness continues or the other person doesn't even respond, then you can smile and let it go. The other person will appreciate it and your conversation will have ended on a good note.

You can also use this opportunity to exit the conversation gracefully if you no longer want to have it. Use the silence to excuse yourself or suddenly remember something you have to do. Don't make a big deal about it. Just smile and thank the person for talking with you. Possibly exchange contact information. Then say, "Excuse me" and move on. Especially do this at parties or networking events, where you have lots of people to talk to and no time for awkward silences. Remember, you always make someone remember how you made them feel, so don't leave the conversation rudely and make the other person feel as if he or she did something wrong. With politeness and warmness, you can leave the person feeling good about the conversation and liking you even more.

Use the time offered by an awkward silence to think of a new topic or a way to phrase a story. It can be related or unrelated to what you were talking about previously. You may also ask a question to start a new line of conversation. Some people are afraid to start new topics because they feel that they are being rude. But clearly, the old topic has died out. Coming up with a new one will be a blessing to the other person as well as you. You just took the burden off the other person to find something to talk about. I often like to end awkward silences by saying, "So, did I ever tell you this story?" Then I launch into a story about something totally bizarre but amusing that happened to me. It always works.

Even better, think back to the conversation and think of a valid question. "So, you mentioned that you study aeronautics. Can you describe that a bit more? I know nothing about it." This is an example that shows you were listening and using the silence to process what you have heard. The other person can appreciate that and fill in more information. The conversation is reborn.

A smooth commentary or joke about the silence can also be useful. Say the silence starts after someone makes a random joke. You can wait a beat, then laugh and say, "I guess none of us can top that!" Or if you have said something that has shocked the other person to silence, say, "I guess I caught you off guard with that zinger. Want to talk about something else?" Or if someone just said something that is difficult to digest, fill the silence with a brief, "I see what you're saying. I'm just taking a moment to think it over."

Watch for someone's body language to see if you

really did make a mistake. You can tell if someone is offended by the way they pull back from you and look displeased, probably just for an instant. You can tell if you made someone uncomfortable judging by an awkward smile and fidgeting or shifting away from you. If you recognize these signs, then apologize. "I said something wrong and I'm sorry. Do you want to talk about something else?"

Sometimes, an awkward silence will ensue when your mind goes blank and you feel unable to think of something to say. Does this sound like a first date you've had? Chances are, nerves have made you unable to be the smooth social charmer you secretly are. The best solution here is to take three consecutive deep breaths through the mouth, exhaling through the nose. Then laugh and make light of your mind going blank.

For example, once I heard a friend of mine discussing how he was unhappy with a grade he had received on one of his college courses. I told him, "Just speak to your...." Then I stopped. The word I was looking for eluded me. An uncomfortable pause stretched on forever and the guy was looking at me, his eyebrows raised. Finally, just as he turned to his partner and started to open his mouth to say something to her, I thought of the word and blurted it out, "Your dean!" Then I laughed and said, "I was having a brain fart." He smiled and the conversation resumed smoothly. A sense of humor about yourself comes in handy in these situations.

Always rehearse a few things to talk about before you meet with someone if your mind tends to go blank during conversation. You will have a reserve of things to talk about if your mind fails to come up with anything on the spot. That can help you navigate uncomfortable pauses as well.

You can have a few go-to questions to start conversations where they have lulled. Consider these:

- Have you always lived in this town?
- If you could live anywhere, where would it be?
- What made you go into [career or field of study]?
- So how did you meet [spouse/partner]?
- What did you think about [major recent event on the news]?
- Did you hear about [some relevant piece of news or local happening]?
- So, tell me more about yourself.
- When did you start working/living here?
- How do you know [mutual friend/host of party/some other person you both know]?

A final tip is to use the silence to your advantage. Therapists call this the "golden rule of silence." If you don't speak, it pressures the other person to fill the silence. In one-on-one conversation, at least. You won't find this trick useful in exchanges with strangers or at parties where people easily lose focus and start talking to someone else. But when you are one-on-one with someone and you find that they are evading a question or refusing to talk, stay silent. The pressure will eventually force them to blurt something out. This is a good way to find out the truth from someone or make someone come up with a new topic to talk about. It is also a good way to get people to start talking about themselves.

How To Have Deeper Conversations

The problem of having deeper conversations is an age-old one. Everyone can engage in small talk. The problem with small talk is that it is not particularly lively and won't stay with you forever. Think back on your most (positive) memorable conversations. They were probably about your philosophy on life, your passions, or something emotional. You probably don't remember too many of those passing "How 'bout them Cowboys?" or "The weather is nice today, isn't it?" conversations.

It is OK to start conversations with some small talk.

After all, small talk serves as an ice breaker that gets you both talking. Use it as your opener and then segue into something more interesting. Be bold and propose any topics you think might be entertaining to both of you.

Listen to what people say. Allow yourself to be vulnerable to their words. If you express emotional reactions to what people say, then you seem more human and take the conversation to a deeper emotional level. For instance, if a woman is talking about how she lost her son, allow yourself to feel sad and show that on your face. "I am so sorry for your loss. You are strong to have gone through that but no one should have to." This is far better than being wooden. You then may mention a major loss you have suffered to show that you understand and you both share something in common.

As people share things, share some things of your own. A woman might talk about her cat, so you talk about how soothing cats are and how they show better health and happiness results in nursing home patients who get to keep cats as pets. A man may mention golf, so you mention how relaxing golf is and talk about some of the courses in town. The conversation just went from small talk to a related deeper subject matter.

Pick a topic you'd like to get deep about in your mind. Then ask a specific question to get the other person to think about said topic. You might say, "So you mentioned you work in a hospital. What is your opinion on the current healthcare crisis?" Or you might say, "So what do you think happened to create us? Do you believe in the Big Bang, or do you think something else happened?"

Ask people about their lives. If someone is talking about his career, you can keep it small talk by asking, "So do you like your job?" Or you can take it deeper by asking, "How does your job make you feel? What are the high and low points?" If someone mentions that she is not sure what she's doing with her life now as she's between jobs, ask, "Where do you see your life headed?" Think about what someone has said and then ask a question that invites introspection and deeper discourse on the matter.

I often love to start a conversation by saying, "I was walking here today and I was really looking at [some building or monument]. It made me think about how it was built and all the lives it has impacted, all the people who have lived or worked there, all the people who have visited it, all the people who have seen it. That gets pretty mind-boggling. How many people do you think have interacted with that place somehow?" Bringing up history and sociology of places is a great way to start a deep, fascinating discussion.

I will do the same thing when looking at the stars with someone. "It's amazing that most of these stars are dead and new ones have been born that we can't see yet because the light hasn't reached us. These stars are millions of years old. What do you think the night sky looks like now?" Looking to the sky and talking about how fascinating it is can really open up conversations on a deeper level.

If you don't want to get philosophical with someone, at least get into politics or religion. Otherwise, you can get into deeper aspects of their personal lives. People are more willing to disclose personal details the more they talk. As they share, listen well and ask questions about how they feel, or empathize.

How To Gracefully End Conversations

A conversation has lost its luster and now you want to talk to someone else. Maybe it's time to get going. How do you politely extract yourself from a conversation without hurting the other person? Some people tend to view it as a rejection when you end the conversation. But most people will understand and not view it as a rejection if you handle the exit carefully.

The best way to end a conversation gracefully is to find a reasonable excuse to leave it. Ask for directions to the restroom, even if you know where it is. Say that you have to call home. Mention that you have to get up early and must go home. Find some reason that you need to go. People may not take a hint, but if you walk away as you say your excuse, they will know the conversation is over. Be sure to say good-bye and thank you for talking or talk again soon as you leave.

Sometimes, you have no desire to end a conversation, but you have other people to talk to. This is especially true at a party or networking mixer. Ask the person to introduce you to other people in the party. Say, "Who else should I meet here?" Or even be honest and say, "It was great talking to you! Here's my number so we can talk again. Now I need to go mingle." Be sure to smile at the person again every time you see him or her at the party.

You can also reverse this by introducing the person to someone you know. They will start talking and you can smile and walk away. You just passed your conversation off on someone else. You will not look as rude walking away. Plus, you may have just brought two people together who will really like each other. You never know.

Another trick at a party or event is to say, "I'm going to refresh my drink. Do you want something?" The other person nearly always says no, so you are free to go to the bar for a drink and then move on. But if the person says yes, get him or her a drink and say, "It was great talking to you. Have a great night." Then hand them the drink and walk away with a big smile.

If your co-worker or fellow student has you trapped in an endless conversation, you can use work or schoolwork as an excuse. "Well, I have to go get this done. Thanks for chatting and I'll see you later!" You just politely closed the conversation and gave a good reason. The other person should not feel rebuffed at all.

When you meet someone, the conversation will eventually have to close. All good things must end. But that doesn't have to be the end of all interaction. Plan a get-together based on some hobby you both share or invite the person to a party or barbecue you may be hosting soon. Even just say, "Let's get together soon" and then hand the person your card or number. Invite someone to connect on social media. Say, "It was so nice talking to you. If you'd like to talk again, this is my number or you can find me on Facebook." You may even pull out your own phone and have them put in their number or help them find you on social media. You can ask them for their card, too. All of these things ensure a future connection that means the conversation did not go to waste. Plus, you make the person feel better about you exiting the conversation because you clearly want to talk again.

Of course, you don't always have to follow up on these

connections. You can ask for their card or number but never contact them again if you don't want to. Asking for contact information is simply a polite way to end the conversation on a positive note.

When you have exited a conversation at a party or work or some other situation with lots of people, be sure to say good-bye to everyone you talked to before you leave. This leaves a warm feeling with the people you met. You don't seem like you're running away, but rather just leaving because it's time to go.

Now sometimes people will be rude. How do you leave a conversation with someone who is insulting you? That is when you need to be assertive. "I don't appreciate what you are saying and I'm going to walk away now." That's all you have to say. Then walk away. Don't engage anymore. There is no justification for an argument; you probably won't win and you will look bad to others if you stand there arguing with someone. So just leave the conversation.

Other people are rude in that they refuse to listen to your cues and let you walk away. They essentially trap you in conversation. Out of a desire to be polite, you keep hinting that you want to leave, but you can't. Even when you start to walk away, they follow, still talking. In these instances, you should also be assertive. "I really need to go now. Nice talking to you!" Then walk away as fast as possible.

Some people don't intend to be rude but they have no social skills and thus can't pick up on social hints. An example may be someone suffering from autism, or someone who grew up isolated. Don't judge this person or be rude to him or her. Just say, "OK, well I really enjoyed talking to you. I have to go, but thanks for chatting. I hope the rest of your day goes well." Redirection also works well with these types. "I've loved talking to you, but maybe we should go do this instead now?" A gentle prompt to do something else can help you extricate yourself from the conversation.

When A Friend Uses You As A Security Blanket Or Vice Versa

In new situations, people get nervous. They tend to want to hang onto a security blanket. This could be you, hanging onto a friend at a party or new social club. It could be your friend, hanging onto you. The problem with using someone as a security blanket is that you smother the person you are using and you prevent both parties from meeting new people. This can lead to a lot of awkwardness, resentment, and missed opportunities.

Social proof means that if you have a friend with you, you are more likely to make other people want to like you [5]. Basically, by having someone like you, you signal to others that you are likable. More people will follow suit. Consider what happens if you go to a bar alone versus when you go with friends. More people will talk to you if you are in a group, but if you are alone, you might get a few glances but few interactions. This is the principle of social proof at play.

But people tend to overuse and rely on social proof too heavily. In new social situations, they cling to their friends, hoping that their friends will help them navigate the social scene. By doing this, they close themselves off to new opportunities to meet others. They zero in on one person and exclude the rest. If you are using someone as a security blanket, or someone is using you, then you need to end the co-dependency and cut you both free to meet new people.

You should be sure to talk to other people. As you stand with your friend, smile at and greet others. Ask your friend to introduce you to people she or he may know and then start conversations with them. Hang out with these new people for a while until the conversation dies. You can then circulate and meet new people. Touch base with your friend occasionally, since you are here together. Probably every two conversations, you can return to your friend without appearing needy or clingy.

In the event that a friend is clinging to you, start introducing him or her to other people. Then walk away as they start talking. Encourage your friend to mingle if he or she keeps following you around. Understand that your friend is probably feeling very out of place and uncomfortable, so ease him or her by making introductions and including him or her in group discussions.

It is perfectly possible to stick with your friend through an entire social event. Just engage in lots of group conversations and invite other people to talk with you. If your friend is engrossed in conversation with someone, don't constantly interrupt. Find someone else to talk to. Often, group conversations tend to splinter into several smaller conversations, so find someone in the group to chat with yourself. If your friend constantly interrupts you while you talk to someone, invite his or her thoughts and try to make them a part of the conversation you are having with someone else.

You may also make a pact before entering a party to mingle. "We need to meet new people tonight, so let's split up and mingle." This sets boundaries from the start to prohibit clinginess.

How To Talk To Someone Who Is Surrounded By Friends

You may experience the flip side of the issue discussed in the previous chapter: You want to talk to someone, but he or she has a security blanket, or is surrounded by a throng of people. Breaking into that throng just to single out the one person you want to talk to can be nerve-wracking and even unwelcome by the other person.

The first method is to wait for the person to break away from the group. You can then catch this person and ask him or her a question to break the ice. You may also offer to get the person something to drink.

This could take forever, however. And you don't want to stop someone who leaves a group conversation to use the bathroom or talk to someone else specific. You want to instead try to enter the group and talk to them as a whole. Walk up to the group and warmly introduce yourself. Mention, "I heard you talking about [blank]." That way, you can enter the group conversation. Start to focus more on the person you are interested in and ask him or her a direct question. Eventually, if you pay enough attention to him or her, you may allow a one-on-one conversation to form and you can splinter off from the group conversation.

This second method is great at parties, where lots of people are mingling and talking in groups. But it may not work in a group of friends spending time together at a bar. The friends may want to be left alone. A good ice breaker may be to walk up to the person you want to speak to and say, "Hey, I noticed you and wanted to say hi." The person may shoot you down, or he or she may want to talk. It is really hit or miss.

You can also use someone's friends to get to them. As you see one of his or her friends alone, mention, "Who is that [person]? Can you tell him/her hi for me?" Another trick is to send a drink to the person in the group, and then smile and wave when the bartender tells the person who bought the drink. This may cause the person to want to talk to you, but again, this is highly hit or miss.

If you are in a group of friends and you see someone in another group of friends, invite the two groups to join. Go over and challenge them to a game of pool at a bar or invite them to share your table. This can make the situation less awkward since more people are involved. You are not doing this alone.

How To Let Someone Know How You Feel About Them

Say you are having the conversation of your life with someone. You want the relationship to go a certain direction, perhaps a romantic one, or perhaps a friendly one. How do you make it clear how you really feel and what you want without seeming forward or weird?

The key to being an adult is clearly communicating what you want with other people. You save a lot of time by making your intentions clear from the start. However, telling a person you just met, "I think I want to date you. How does that sound?" can grind the conversation to a very terrible stop. There are unique connections where this kind of phrase will work beautifully, but generally, this kind of directness will only make others uncomfortable.

You can state your intentions without being too direct. Say you meet someone at a singles mixer and you have romantic intent. You can say, "I am looking for someone to date." If a person meets you at a random place and asks what you are looking for, be honest without saying specifically, "I want to date you." Then ask the other person what they want. If they want the same thing as you, say, "Would you be interested in seeing me again?" Even if the person says no, you can gain brownie points by giving him or her your card or number and saying, "Well, in case you change your mind, you can call me."

At the end of a great conversation, you can say, "I really enjoyed hanging out with you. I'd love to see you again. What do you think?"

Sometimes, two people are magnetic. This can be true for couples or friends. You meet and without a doubt you like each other. It is clear in both of your words, facial expressions, and body language. In this case, go with social cues. "I think we should be friends. Let me get your number." "I think we should go out sometime."

A first date is an ideal time to state your intentions. Be clear if you are looking for something serious or casual. People will know what you mean, and if they don't, clarify. You don't want to lead someone on or create confusion by being unclear about your intentions. A lot of drama can be avoided and someone will respect you more if you just say what you want off the bat. It's perfectly acceptable to be assertive and say, "I'm not looking for anything serious right now." Don't just say what you think someone wants to hear because you may be wrong. You may be surprised that another person wants the same thing as you. If the other person wants something else, then now they know what you want and how to proceed.

If you are simply not sure where you want the relationship to go, then you don't have to say anything. Just invite the person to talk to you more. Take your time getting to the person until you decide. If the person ever asks, "What do you want from me?" or some such question, be honest that you are not sure right now. Ask for more time to get to know the person and invite him or her to share more about him- or herself.

A lot of people feel the need to make excuses for what they want. "I'm not looking for something serious because I got hurt recently." "I want a serious relationship because I'm already 35 and still not married." "I don't seem to do well in relationships so I just like to sleep around." There is no need to make excuses unless the other person asks. Just state your intentions and leave it at that. You don't need to explain yourself. Most people don't even want to know the details.

You may find yourself in a situation where you decide not to pursue a relationship of any kind with someone. Be as direct as possible and you will avoid hurt feelings. Say something simple and concise, like, "I don't see this going anywhere" or "I think we're better suited for other people." Lying can only lead to more heartache in the future.

Perhaps you meet a girl and you don't want to date her. You tell her that you are not interested in something serious to gently reject her. But then you meet another girl and you fall in love. The first girl later finds out and is devastated that you lied. She would be less hurt if you had simply told her, "I just don't feel a connection with you. I am going to see other people." It will hurt at first, but she will not feel lied to.

When Someone Is Trying To Argue With You Or Has To Be Right

Some people just have to be right at all times. They will argue themselves blue in the face. Dale Carnegie says that the best argument is the one you never have [11]. In other words, don't engage with these people because it is not worth it and you won't win.

If you stand there and argue with someone, then you anger that person. You also look bad to those around you. You should pick your battles and walk away from ones that are not going to bring any value to your life. Most arguments are not worth having. You don't need to be right any more than the other person does. Only harm will come from engaging.

When a person tries to be right, let them. You won't convince them otherwise. Just nod and agree to disagree.

If a person becomes confrontational, let that person look like a fool in front of everyone else. Smile and say, "I don't want to argue right now." Change the subject or use that chance to walk away. You will have saved yourself some face.

When Someone Asks Or Says Inappropriate Things

Have you ever had someone ask you something really personal or just generally inappropriate? Some people advise that you redirect uncomfortable questions back to the asker. But this is actually bound to backfire. Any person who is comfortable asking uncomfortable questions is also comfortable answering them. If you direct the question back to the person, he or she will likely give you details that you didn't want to know.

Instead, practice your assertiveness skills by assertively ending the line of inappropriate questioning. When your nosy co-worker asks about your divorce, for instance, just smile and say, "I really don't want to talk about that." Then change the subject or walk away. You are creating boundaries this way, showing others what is and what is not OK to talk about with you.

If someone says something really inappropriate to

you, just say something like, "That is not appropriate. I don't want to talk about this." You should use this with people who repeatedly bring up inappropriate things or people who are flirting with you. Really, you should use this whenever you feel someone is making you uncomfortable. State that you want to talk about something else or move along. There is no need to keep up a conversation with someone who has no sense of boundaries.

However, some people just don't know any better. A small child does not know that it is rude to ask someone if she is pregnant, for instance. Have some tolerance for these people and gently smile as you tell them, "That is not appropriate to say or to ask people." You just taught someone a valuable life lesson.

When Someone Embarrasses You

We have all been through these moments. A drunk friend humiliates you in front of a person you have a crush on. A family member busts out the photo album full of naked baby pictures of you when you bring your boyfriend or girlfriend over for the first time. A particularly mean co-worker reminds everyone how you failed at a big launch, incurring mean-spirited laughter all around. Someone makes a hurtful joke about you that fails to be funny.

Often, people put you down in public to make themselves feel better. It is a symptom of their own low self-esteem. This can lead to serious social anxiety and mimics symptoms of PTSD in people who have been humiliated [18]. It is a form of emotional abuse that can make you hate social situations. However, just remember that not everyone does this and most people won't even remember what your mean-spirited bully said about you. Even if they do, they probably agree that this person was out of line, but they don't say so to avoid being bullied themselves. Also remember that this behavior is your friend's self-esteem problem, not your own issue.

Someone may also embarrass you without meaning to. A well-intentioned comment that ends up being insulting, a slip of a secret, or some drunken behavior aimed at you is typically not meant to be humiliating. Accept that this humiliation was accidental and

The first thing to do is to look at the person who embarrassed you and say, "Why did you just say that?" This puts them on the spot and tells them that this behavior is not acceptable. It also makes others respect you because you stood up for yourself.

Then you can do one of two things: Walk away and talk to other people or change the subject. Which option you choose is up to you and the level of humiliation you feel. Either way, you save face.

When You Say The Wrong Thing

Since no one on Earth is perfect, we have certainly all

said the wrong thing at some time or another. We either deeply angered or hurt a friend or made a complete stranger uncomfortable. Then we agonize in humiliation for years after, replaying the conversation in our minds and thinking about how we should have done things differently. This is actually normal [18].

Truthfully, you cannot change the past. Kicking yourself over something you said is useless. Instead, take ownership of what you said and try to fix it right after you say it. Give yourself a chance to make things right in the moment.

First, always acknowledge that you said the wrong thing. Even if no one comments on it, they have noticed. You will look bad if you just let it slide. You are not off the hook just because no one speaks up. Instead, say, "I'm so sorry. Can I take that back?"

You may need to give a person space and time if you

really said something horrible. Apologize and then ask the person to forgive you. Leave him or her alone for a while. Wait for him or her to reach out to you. You may consider touching base in a week or two to say sorry again.

Never pin the blame for what you said on others. You might be tempted to tell someone that he is too sensitive for getting offended at a joke you told about him, for instance. That's a form of emotional abuse. Instead, take full responsibility for what you said. "That was wrong of me and I shouldn't have said that."

Don't offer excuses or justifications of your behavior. Nothing you can say will make it right except an apology. By making excuses, you appear to be saying, "I didn't really do anything wrong."

If you say something embarrassing, just make light of it. Laugh at yourself and say, "That was a dumb thing to say. Let me try again." This helps other people laugh along with you and give you another chance to save face.

When You Can't Think Of A Response

Someone just dropped a real bombshell mid-conversation. Now your mind is reeling and you don't know what to say. This can be awkward.

Maybe someone is teasing you and you can't think of a comeback. In this case, just laugh or say, "Wow, that was a good one. I can't even think of a response." Make light of your blank mind to ease the awkwardness of the situation.

Or maybe someone said something powerful. Just say, "Wow. I need a moment to process that" or "That really moved me. Give me a second to think about it." Take a few deep breaths to clear your mind. Then you will likely think of something.

If someone said something grossly inappropriate or offensive, you can give them a look and walk away. This shows them that they can't speak that way to you. But it can also end any chance of future conversations. To be politer, you can just say, "That was not appropriate, now was it?" This admonishes the person without being too harsh.

When people share painful things with you, most people say, "I'm sorry." This is not a helpful response. It is far better to say, "Is there anything I can do?" Most people just want you to listen. You can listen and nod sympathetically. Say something like, "You must feel [blank]" to encourage someone to talk about his or her feelings. You should also compliment someone on their strength getting through a tragedy or other problem.

Don't apologize and don't offer advice or opinions that no one asked for. These comments are always unwelcome. It is also unwelcomed if you immediately jump to talking about yourself. While you may think you know what this person is going through because you have been through something similar, you don't really know what someone is feeling because everyone responds to situations differently. You can say, "I have been through that too and it's rough" just to create a sense of similarity and make the person feel less alone. But don't wax poetic on what happened to you, taking the spotlight away. That is selfish. Instead, focus the conversation back on the other person and let the person get his troubles off of his chest in his own way.

It is not your job in life to play therapist to everyone. If you don't feel like hearing about someone's troubles, you can offer a sympathetic response and hug, then move along by changing the subject.

Sometimes, you don't need to think of a response. Just reflect what you feel with your facial expression.

Show that you are listening with a nod or a touch on the arm. Give a person a hug. You don't always need to be full of answers and witticisms. No one will think less of you for having nothing valuable to say at certain times in the conversation.

You can also fill this mind blank with reflective listening. Just repeat what someone said to give yourself time to process it. You can paraphrase to save time and effort. This makes it sound like you have a response and encourage the other person to keep talking. Meanwhile, you don't have to think of anything to say.

Refrain from making a bad joke or rambling to fill the awkward pause that may come with your inability to respond. That just makes you draw negative attention to yourself. You will look far more respectable if you stay quiet than if you say something dumb.

Hanging Out With New People Who All Know Each Other

A super common and nerve-wracking situation is when you find yourself in a group of people who all know each other. These people are too busy exchanging inside jokes and catching up to pay you much mind. You can feel very out of place.

The first step is to relax. Nerves will prevent you from ever breaking down the barriers you have with these people. They don't know you and they are preoccupied with their other friends. They will overlook you and they are not judging you as much as you think.

Next, try to become part of the group. Don't just be a silent wallflower, standing by the wall and listening without talking. Listen to what people say and respond. Inject yourself in the conversation. Try to find things in common with these people.

Ask them questions, like, "How long have you guys all known each other?" People will love sharing the histories of their friendships. If they all engage in a certain hobby, ask them questions about why they got into this hobby and if that's how they all know each other.

As this group of friends shares things you can't talk about, such as memories, other people in the group you don't know, or inside jokes, you don't need to pretend to keep up. You are an outsider and you are not expected to know what they are talking about. Just smile and wait for the topic to turn. Or propose a topic yourself.

Don't ask traditional questions to get to know everyone. The group will not be receptive to this. Instead, talk like you already know them and participate in the conversations the group has. Talk about whatever the group wants to talk about. Add some stories or jokes that fit in line with what the group is talking about so they can get to know you.

Be friendly to everyone, not just a few people. Even if you get bad impressions of certain members of the group, remember that you are only getting a small snapshot of who they really are. If you are friendly, you make a good impression. Not everyone may like you, but you won't walk away with any enemies.

It may take a few times for a group to warm up to you. The more times they see you and talk to you, the more welcome they will make you feel in the future. Keep coming around. You will eventually be accepted. If, however, you don't seem to share anything in common with the group and you don't have to see them again, feel free to never return to that particular group setting.

When Everyone Is Talking About A Topic You Can't Contribute To

You don't know everything in the world. You may often run into conversations about things you don't know anything about. Don't pretend to know. Express interest instead and listen well.

You may also ask, "Can you guys explain this to me?" Someone may be happy to explain the topic to you. You can also do quick research on your phone in order to participate.

Another tactic is to wait until the conversation appears to be winding down and then propose a new topic you do know about. Don't interrupt a conversation in full swing with some random subject change, as that will be unwelcome. But when people seem to be running out of things to say, you are welcome to introduce a new subject.

How To Respond To "You're So Quiet"

When someone says this, your first instinct may be to explain your behavior. But this is not necessary. You don't have to explain or excuse who you are.

You exude confidence when you own your personality. Just smile and say, "Yes, I'm a quiet person." Brush off this comment because it doesn't really mean anything. It is not usually intended as an insult. Most people use it as a sort of ice breaker, because they can't think of anything to say to the quiet person. Use that ice breaker as a chance to start talking and get a conversation going.

When People Aren't Interested In Talking About Your Hobbies

Not everyone is going to care about your Star Trek club or your favorite sport. When you can't talk about hobbies, what can you talk about? The truth is that hobbies are certainly not the center of the universe and you don't have to talk about them. Most books on conversations drill talking about hobbies into you, and while this is definitely a great topic to propose to find something in common with someone, it fails when your conversation partner has no interest in your interests.

Instead of feeling rebuffed or rejected, accept that not everyone has the same interests in life as you do. Try to find other topics to talk about. Ask the person about his hobbies and compare and contrast them to your own. Or simply switch the subject entirely to current events, work, or the person's life.

When You Are Not Interested In What Someone Has To Say

Nothing is duller than a conversation with someone you don't find interesting. The key here is learning to gracefully change the subject or end the conversation. Since you already know how to end the conversation, let's discuss how to change the subject.

An abrupt subject change signals that you don't share an interest in what the person is saying, which can hurt the other person. Since you are supposed to express interest in others in conversation, you should pretend to be interested. Nod, make a nice comment about what the person says, and listen for a few minutes. When the person pauses, you can find a relevant subject change somewhat related to what he or she was saying.

For instance, if someone is going on and on about rocket science and you don't care, you can take advantage of a lull in the conversation to say, "I always wanted to be an astronaut as a kid. I'd love to explore outer space." It is somewhat related, so it doesn't throw a person off. But it also redirects the conversation.

You may also say, "I don't know anything about that, really. I'm more of a sports guy." That way, you politely tell the person what you are more interested in talking about. He or she may take the bait or may not.

When People Don't Ask About You In Conversations

In this book and in many others on the topic of conversation, you have undoubtedly read the advice to talk about other people. This is a foolproof way to get people to talk, since they love talking about themselves. The kicker is that these books encourage an ebb and flow of talking about yourself and asking about someone else. They assume the other person will ask you questions about yourself or at least somehow try to get to know you. But any person who has had real-life conversations knows that this is not how a large number of conversations go. Many people are self-absorbed or simply don't have the social skills to ask you about yourself, so they monopolize the conversation talking about themselves or droning on about some topic they fancy themselves to be experts in. The result is that you may feel as if your conversational partner is not interested in you as a person, which can sting your ego.

When this happens often, you start to ask yourself if you are doing something to put people off. You may feel like no one cares. Or you may even feel that everyone in this world is selfish.

Stop for a moment and consider the conversations you have had that you can remember. Did every single one of them go this way, or are you selectively remembering? You may be choosing to focus on the negative ones because people tend to focus on the negative experiences they have more than the positive ones [12]. Even rats tend to focus more on the bad than the good in clinical studies and people all tend to do this [12]. The truth is that more people ask about you than you realize, and you just focus on the few selfish ones that do not.

The harsh truth is that if this happens to you in every

conversation, you may be at fault. You are not showing people that you are interesting. Thus, they gloss over you, not caring about what you have to say. The easiest way to get over this hump is to interject the other person's monologue with something interesting, find interesting tidbits about yourself to mention regarding what they are saying, or even wear something interesting that invites conversation. Also, raise your voice a bit. Quiet voices tend to get drowned out and overlooked in conversation. Speak first and speak fast.

But it may not be your fault – in fact, it probably isn't. Many people are just more concerned with themselves than others and lack the social skills to even pretend to care about others. You are not boring, but this person finds everyone else besides himself or herself boring. You will find that no matter what you say, this person ignores you or finds a way to twist the conversation back to himself or herself.

There is also often social context to consider. If a group of people is chatting, they tend to not to ask direct questions of you, but rather talk amongst themselves about something in general. A large group of friends does not have the time to catch up with every single other person, preferring to talk together about general topics. You may have better luck getting people to ask about you in one-on-one situations.

People doing activities together tend to discuss the activity at hand, not ask each other questions. They want to get the task done. This is especially true for new activities, where people don't know you. Consider a new group playing tennis. Everyone is focused on the game, not you. No one is going to try to get to know you until the game is over. The end of the game is a good time to strike up some one-on-one conversations as you wash up, pack up, and walk out to your cars.

During certain meetings or get-togethers, people talk about the usual topics, instead of each other. For instance, at an office party, people may be more interested in talking about work and their bosses than asking you about yourself. Conversations often focus on the thing that people have the most in common. A work meeting would be comprised of people who have work in common. Don't take it personally. People who work together may catch up with a good work buddy or two, but they are not going to ask you all about how your life is going.

At parties, people are under the influence and more self-involved, far more interested in what they have to say rather than how you are. Bars and clubs are the same way. Often, these situations don't invite highly personal conversations anyway, since they are loud and crowded and distracting. Don't focus too much on how someone acts when they are in a different state of mind or in party mode.

You may find yourself in situations where you are out of place and so no one feels a connection to you and doesn't experience the need to ask you about yourself. Often, your confidence is poor in these situations because you know you're the odd man out. Your lack of confidence can be off-putting. Try to smile more and be more laidback. Crack a few jokes and don't expect to be the center of attention.

Finally, on situations where the other person is trying to impress you, such as a date or job interview, they may make the mistake of talking only about themselves as an attempt to "sell" themselves to you. Just listen and wait for a chance to talk about yourself. You may have to inject yourself into the conversation. Obviously, this behavior indicates poor social skills and low self-esteem in the other person, who wants to please you to feel confident; you can use this to consider if you want to see this person again.

Consider the conversational style of the person you

are talking to, as well. Many people don't like to waste time on small talk and expect you to bring up things about yourself without being asked. This is incredibly common, actually. You should bring up things about yourself without being asked. Bring up things that are relevant and related to what the other person is saying. Show your confidence by being willing to share things about yourself without any prodding from others.

If you do say about yourself and no one acts interested, don't let that get you down. Especially in large groups, you may just not stand out at a particular moment. Try to find more things to say that seem suited for the social situation at hand and keep trying until you get a response. Staying relevant plays to the interests of the other person, making you seem more intriguing.

In one-on-one conversations, if you continually talk about yourself and still feel that the other person is ignoring you or disinterested in you, this indicates poor social skills on the part of the other person. Watch how they are with others and see if they are the same way to everyone. Even if they act more interest in other people, their rudeness to you shows that no relationship is possible. You should just excuse yourself from these conversations and move on. A million better conversation partners exist out there.

Conclusion

Hacks make everything in life easier. Therefore, when it comes to something as challenging as learning social skills later in life, having some hacks in your back pocket can be life-saving. You can dig yourself out of any awkward or humiliating situation, approach unapproachable people, and turn enemies into friends. There is really nothing you can't do with some solid social skill hacks.

Social skills are imperative to operating at your full potential in life. You can make anything go your way if you know how to handle people properly. The hacks in this book will help you handle any situation that may arise smoothly and without mishap.

No one likes an awkward conversation. It can sour your mood and the entire interaction. But now you won't have to worry about that because you know the secrets to avoid and end awkwardness.

Superficial conversations are also annoying and they

fail to lead to any depth in the relationship. Now you know how to skip the small talk in favor of more profound discussions that lead to more heartfelt connections. Imagine elevating conversations from talking about the weather to discussing your ideas about how to save the Earth from an asteroid or some similar fascinating topic that really shows your personality and the other person's thoughts.

You have also learned how to ask for what you want. You cannot expect to get things if you don't ask, so always ask. You have learned how to gracefully respond to the word "no" and turn negatives into positives. Imagine the doors you can open in life if you start asking for what you want and getting it!

Praising people sparks their passion for talking to you. So, does asking the right questions. You have learned how to open communication, instead of allowing it to come to a dead end. Open-ended questions, relevant conversational shifts, and other such techniques keep conversations from growing stale and then dying out.

Many people make the mistake of focusing on their problems, their visions, and their desires in conversation. Now you know better. You know that to really appeal to people, you must show them how they benefit and how they can get what they want. Only then can you truly inspire and convince people. Only then will you make sensational speeches and appeals that grip people, getting them to come around to your way of thinking.

Enthusiasm, new words, and new topics are all essential ways to get people to like you more. But you can use sneaky hacks from NLP and cognitive behavioral therapy to crack conversations open and turn them from mundane exchanges to dynamic ones. You will certainly be memorable now that you start using these hacks!

Since these hacks will elevate your social life to new

heights, you should start using them today. Practice makes perfect, so starting to use these now will cement them as regular staples of your social interactions. Soon you won't even have to think about them, you will just do them. Your life will improve exponentially as you begin to deal with people in a more satisfying way.

References

1. Hasson, Uri. Clicking: How Our Brains are in Sync. Princeton. https://www.princeton.edu/news/2011/12/05/hasson-brings-real-life-lab-examine-cognitive-processing

2. Putz, Ole. How Strangers Initiate Conversations: Interactions on Public Trains in Germany. Sage Journals. 2017. DOI: https://doi.org/10.1177/0891241617697792.

3. Carolyn Parkinson, Adam M. Kleinbaum, & Thalia Wheatley. Similar neural responses predict friendship. Journal of Nature Communications, Vol 9, Article # 332. 2018.

4. Yoshimoto, S. et al. (2014). Pupil Response and the Subliminal Mere Exposure Effect. PLOS One. 9(2): e90670. doi: 10.1371/journal.pone.0090670

5. Cialdini, R. (2008). Influence: The Psychology of Persuasion, 5th Ed. Allyn and Bacon. ISBN-13: 9 78-0061241895

6. Maslow, A. H. (1943). A theory of human motivation. Psychological Review, 50(4), 370-396. http://dx.doi.org/10.1037/h0054346

7. Tesser, M. Advanced Social Psychology. New York: McGraw Hill.

8. Deluga, R.J. Supervisor Trust Building, Leader-Member Exchange, and Organizational Citizenship Behavior. Journal of Occupational and Organizational Psychology. Vol 67, pp. 315-326.

9. Gravagna, Nicole. Question Askers Versus Open Sharers: How Different Conversation Styles Interact. Huffington Post. https://www.huffpost.com/entry/question-

askers-and-open-sharers-how-different-conversation_b_59c5e5d7e4b08d66155042ad.

10. Apperle, Robin, et al. Neural responses to maternal praise and criticism: Relationship to depression and anxiety symptoms in high-risk adolescent girls. Neuroimage Clin. 2016; 11: 548–554. Published online 2016 Apr 4. doi: 10.1016/j.nicl.2016.03.009.

11. Carnegie, Dale. How to Win Friends and Influence People. Pocket Books. 1998. ISBN-13: 978-0671027032.

12. Baumeister, F., et al. Bad Is Stronger than Good. Review of General Psychology, 2001. Vol 5, No 4, pp. 323-370. DOI: 10.1037//1089-2680.5.4.323

13. Kini, P., et al. The Effects of Gratitude Expression on Neural Activity. Neorimage. 2016 Mar;128:1-

10. doi: 10.1016/j.neuroimage.2015.12.040. Epub 2015 Dec 30.

14. Mueller, P. & Oppenheimer, D.M. The Pen Is Mightier than the Keyboard: Advantages of Longhand Over Laptop Note-Taking. Association for Psychological Science. 2014. Vol 25, No 6, pp. 1159-1168. DOI: 10.1177/0956797614524581

15. Adam D. I. Kramer, Jamie E. Guillory, and Jeffrey T. Hancock. Experimental evidence of massive-scale emotional contagion through social networks. PNAS. 2014. Vol 111, Issue 24, pp. 8788-8790.
https://doi.org/10.1073/pnas.1320040111

16. Aron, Arthur, et al. The Experimental Generation of Interpersonal Closeness: A Procedure and Some   Findings.
https://journals.sagepub.com/doi/pdf/10.1177/01 46167297234003.

17. Koudenburg, N., Postmes, T., & Gordijin, E.H. Disrupting the Flow: How Brief Silences In Group Conversations Affect Social Needs. Journal of Experimental Social Psychology. 2011. https://www.rug.nl/staff/n.koudenburg/koudenb urgetal.2011.pdf.

18. Torres, Walter & Bergner, Raymond. Humiliation: Its Nature and Consequences. Journal of the American Academy of Psychiatry and the Law. 2010. Vol 38, No 2, pp. 195-204.

Disclaimer

The information contained in this book and its components, is meant to serve as a comprehensive collection of strategies that the author of this book has done research about. Summaries, strategies, tips and tricks are only recommendations by the author, and reading this book will not guarantee that one's results will exactly mirror the author's results.

The author of this book has made all reasonable efforts to provide current and accurate information for the readers of this book. The author and its associates will not be held liable for any unintentional errors or omissions that may be found.

The material in the book may include information by third parties. Third party materials comprise of opinions expressed by their owners. As such, the author of this book does not assume responsibility or liability for any third party material or opinions.

The publication of third party material does not

constitute the author's guarantee of any information, products, services, or opinions contained within third party material. Use of third party material does not guarantee that your results will mirror our results. Publication of such third party material is simply a recommendation and expression of the author's own opinion of that material.

Whether because of the progression of the Internet, or the unforeseen changes in company policy and editorial submission guidelines, what is stated as fact at the time of this writing may become outdated or inapplicable later.

Printed in Great Britain
by Amazon